FLORIDA TEST PREP

FAST Practice Test Book

Star Mathematics

Kindergarten

ISBN 9798866088362

TEST MASTER PRESS

CONTENTS

INTRODUCTION
For Parents, Teachers, and Tutors

About the New Florida Assessment of Student Thinking (F.A.S.T.)

Beginning in the 2022-2023 school year, students in Florida will take the Florida Assessment of Student Thinking (F.A.S.T.). This is a Progress Monitoring System that involves taking tests throughout the school year to show current level and progress. Students in Kindergarten will take the Star Mathematics test produced by Renaissance Learning. The tests are taken three times throughout the year. This practice test book will prepare students for the Star Mathematics tests.

About Florida's New Mathematics Standards

Student learning and assessment in Florida is based on the skills listed in the new Benchmarks for Excellent Student Thinking, or B.E.S.T. The mathematics standards are divided into five broad domains, with specific benchmarks within each domain. This practice test book contains at least one question for each benchmark on every practice test.

About the Star Mathematics Tests

The Star Mathematics tests assess math skills by having students answer 34 multiple-choice questions with four answer choices. Students should be able to complete each question within 3 minutes.

Taking the Practice Tests

This book contains four practice tests similar to the real Star Mathematics tests. Each practice test contains 36 questions, and the tests have been divided into three sections of 12 questions each. This allows students to have ongoing practice, and for review and feedback between sessions. A complete test can also be practiced by taking all 3 sessions in a row.

On the real tests, audio is enabled so that the questions can be read to the students. This test can be given to students by reading each question. If students complete the test independently, questions have been written as simply as possible to reduce reading demands.

Practice Test 1

Session 1

Instructions
Read each question carefully.
Each question has four answer choices.
Fill in the circle for the correct answer.

1   How many apples are there?

(A)   5

(B)   6

(C)   7

(D)   8

2   How long is the broom?

(A)   7 units

(B)   8 units

(C)   9 units

(D)   10 units

3   Where is the giraffe?

(A)   first

(B)   second

(C)   third

(D)   fourth

4   Which number is 1 less than 14?

(A)   12

(B)   13

(C)   15

(D)   16

5 There are 6 cupcakes.

Mike eats 2 cupcakes. How many are left?

Ⓐ 2 cupcakes

Ⓑ 4 cupcakes

Ⓒ 5 cupcakes

Ⓓ 8 cupcakes

6 How is the top caterpillar different to the bottom one?

Ⓐ It is shorter.

Ⓑ It is longer.

Ⓒ It is heavier.

Ⓓ It is fuller.

7   Which shape is a sphere?

(A)

(B)

(C)

(D)

8   Which number has 1 ten and 5 ones?

(A)   6

(B)   11

(C)   15

(D)   51

9   How many squares are in the shapes below?

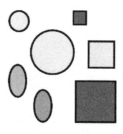

(A) 2

(B) 3

(C) 4

(D) 7

10   What does the picture show?

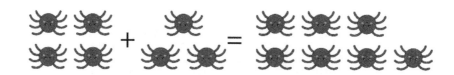

(A) 3 + 3 = 6

(B) 4 + 3 = 7

(C) 4 + 4 = 8

(D) 7 + 3 = 10

11 Which item is most like a circle?

(A) picture

(B) sun

(C) bag

(D) tent

12 What is 2 + 3?

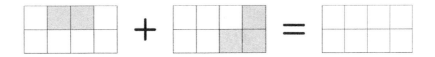

(A) 4

(B) 5

(C) 6

(D) 7

Practice Test 1

Session 2

Instructions

Read each question carefully.

Each question has four answer choices.

Fill in the circle for the correct answer.

13 What number is added to 7 to make 10?

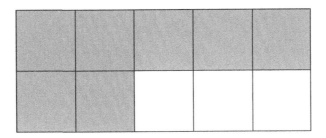

Ⓐ 2

Ⓑ 3

Ⓒ 4

Ⓓ 5

14 There are 4 chairs at a table.

Jim adds two more chairs. How many chairs are there?

Ⓐ 5 chairs

Ⓑ 6 chairs

Ⓒ 7 chairs

Ⓓ 8 chairs

15   What number is 3 more than 4?

(A)   5

(B)   6

(C)   7

(D)   8

16   Which set has six bags?

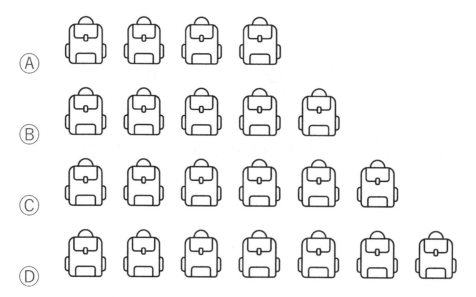

17 In which set are there more cats than dogs?

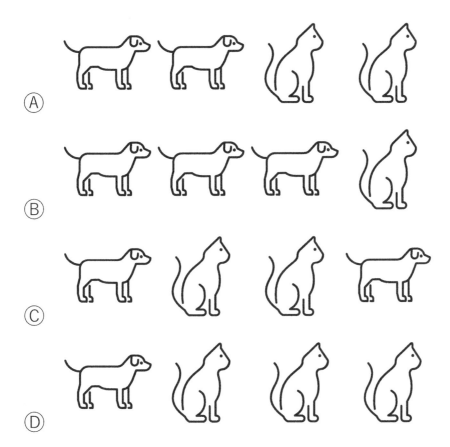

Ⓐ

Ⓑ

Ⓒ

Ⓓ

18 What number comes right after 26?

Ⓐ 24

Ⓑ 25

Ⓒ 27

Ⓓ 28

19 What is this showing about the brush?

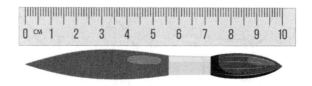

Ⓐ how light it is

Ⓑ how long it is

Ⓒ how much it holds

Ⓓ how much it costs

20 Which shape has fewer sides than a square?

Ⓐ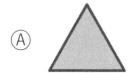

Ⓑ

Ⓒ

Ⓓ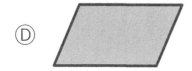

21 Which item is second in the line below?

Ⓐ beetle

Ⓑ lamp

Ⓒ log

Ⓓ sun

22 Which of these shows 5 cows?

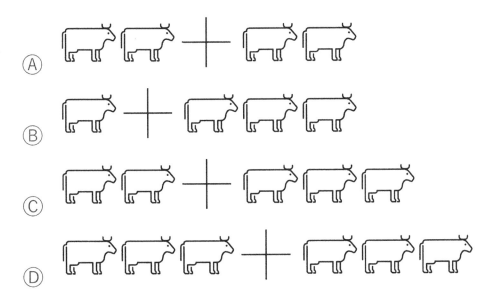

23 What shape is the paint tin?

Ⓐ cone

Ⓑ cylinder

Ⓒ cube

Ⓓ sphere

24 Which two numbers make 5?

Ⓐ 1 and 3

Ⓑ 2 and 3

Ⓒ 2 and 4

Ⓓ 3 and 3

Practice Test 1

Session 3

Instructions

Read each question carefully.

Each question has four answer choices.

Fill in the circle for the correct answer.

---

25 There are 8 carrots. Emma takes 3 away.

How many carrots are left?

Ⓐ 4

Ⓑ 5

Ⓒ 6

Ⓓ 7

26 How many of the cookies below are triangles?

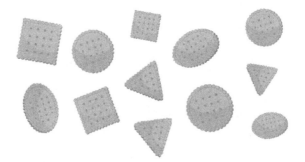

Ⓐ 2

Ⓑ 3

Ⓒ 4

Ⓓ 5

27   How many small squares make up the large square?

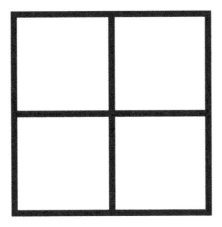

Ⓐ   4

Ⓑ   6

Ⓒ   8

Ⓓ   10

28   Which of these shows 6 bells?

Ⓐ

Ⓑ

Ⓒ

Ⓓ

29 What is being found about the apple?

Ⓐ how long it is

Ⓑ how tall it is

Ⓒ how heavy it is

Ⓓ how full it is

30 Which bottle has the most in it?

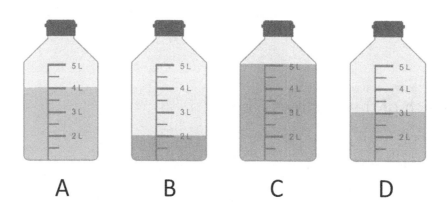

A   B   C   D

Ⓐ Bottle A

Ⓑ Bottle B

Ⓒ Bottle C

Ⓓ Bottle D

31   What shape is shown below?

  Ⓐ   circle

  Ⓑ   rectangle

  Ⓒ   square

  Ⓓ   triangle

32   What is 2 + 4?

  Ⓐ   5

  Ⓑ   6

  Ⓒ   7

  Ⓓ   8

33 Which shape has 2 round faces?

Ⓐ

Ⓑ

Ⓒ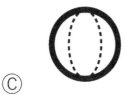

Ⓓ

34 What number do the blocks show?

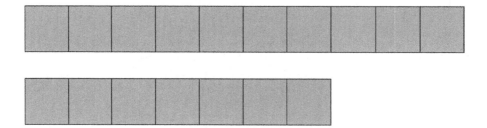

Ⓐ 13

Ⓑ 17

Ⓒ 30

Ⓓ 70

35 Some fish are shown below.

How many fish are there?

Ⓐ 7

Ⓑ 8

Ⓒ 9

Ⓓ 10

36 Which is equal to 10?

Ⓐ 2 + 2

Ⓑ 3 + 3

Ⓒ 4 + 4

Ⓓ 5 + 5

Practice Test 2

Session 1

Instructions
Read each question carefully.
Each question has four answer choices.
Fill in the circle for the correct answer.

1   Some birds are shown below.

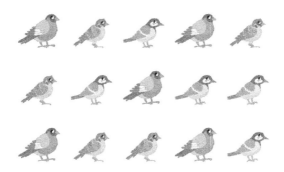

How many birds are there?

Ⓐ   5

Ⓑ   10

Ⓒ   15

Ⓓ   20

2   How tall is the bag?

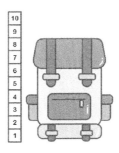

Ⓐ   7 units

Ⓑ   8 units

Ⓒ   9 units

Ⓓ   10 units

3 Where is the kite?

Ⓐ first

Ⓑ second

Ⓒ third

Ⓓ fourth

4 Which number is 1 more than 55?

Ⓐ 54

Ⓑ 56

Ⓒ 58

Ⓓ 59

5   There are 10 frogs on a pond.

Then 4 frogs hop away. How many are left?

Ⓐ   4 frogs

Ⓑ   5 frogs

Ⓒ   6 frogs

Ⓓ   7 frogs

6   How is the top hotdog different to the bottom one?

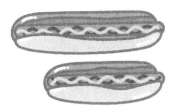

Ⓐ   It is shorter.

Ⓑ   It is longer.

Ⓒ   It weighs less.

Ⓓ   It holds less.

7   Which shape is a cube?

Ⓐ

Ⓑ

Ⓒ

Ⓓ

8   Which number has 1 ten and 6 ones?

Ⓐ 10

Ⓑ 16

Ⓒ 60

Ⓓ 66

9   How many of the buttons below are round?

(A) 3

(B) 4

(C) 5

(D) 6

10   What does the picture show?

(A) 3 − 1 = 2

(B) 4 − 1 = 3

(C) 5 − 1 = 4

(D) 6 − 1 = 5

11 What are all the items shaped like?

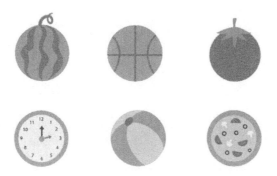

Ⓐ circles

Ⓑ rectangles

Ⓒ squares

Ⓓ triangles

12 What is 4 + 2?

Ⓐ 4

Ⓑ 5

Ⓒ 6

Ⓓ 7

Practice Test 2

Session 2

Instructions

Read each question carefully.

Each question has four answer choices.

Fill in the circle for the correct answer.

13 What number is added to 6 to make 10?

Ⓐ 2

Ⓑ 3

Ⓒ 4

Ⓓ 5

14 May has 4 balls of wool.

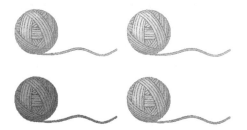

She needs 6 balls of wool to make a scarf. How many more does she need?

Ⓐ 2

Ⓑ 3

Ⓒ 4

Ⓓ 5

15 What number is missing?

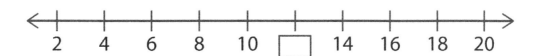

(A) 11

(B) 12

(C) 13

(D) 15

16 Which set has 7 crabs?

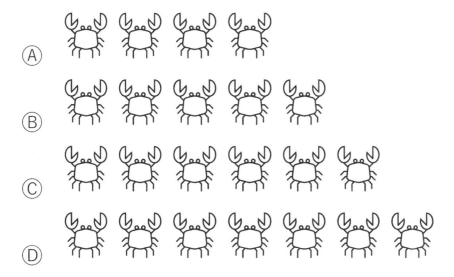

17 In which set are the number of buses and planes equal?

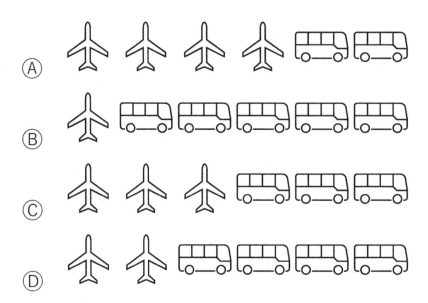

Ⓐ

Ⓑ

Ⓒ

Ⓓ

18 What number comes right before 64?

Ⓐ 62

Ⓑ 63

Ⓒ 65

Ⓓ 66

19 What is this showing about the key?

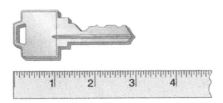

Ⓐ   how heavy it is

Ⓑ   how long it is

Ⓒ   how strong it is

Ⓓ   how shiny it is

20 Which shape has fewer sides than a triangle?

Ⓐ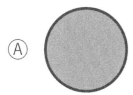

Ⓑ

Ⓒ

Ⓓ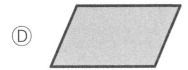

21 Which item is third in the line below?

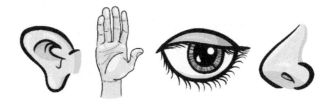

  (A) ear

  (B) hand

  (C) eye

  (D) nose

22 What is equal to 7?

  (A) 2 + 3

  (B) 2 + 4

  (C) 2 + 5

  (D) 2 + 6

23   Which item is shaped like a cube?

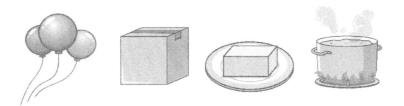

Ⓐ   balloon

Ⓑ   box

Ⓒ   butter

Ⓓ   pot

24   Which two numbers make 7?

Ⓐ   1 and 5

Ⓑ   2 and 6

Ⓒ   3 and 4

Ⓓ   3 and 5

Practice Test 2

Session 3

Instructions

Read each question carefully.

Each question has four answer choices.

Fill in the circle for the correct answer.

25 Leo has 5 apples. He eats 2 apples.

How many apples are left?

Ⓐ 1

Ⓑ 2

Ⓒ 3

Ⓓ 4

26 How many of the items below are shorts?

Ⓐ 3

Ⓑ 4

Ⓒ 5

Ⓓ 6

27 How many small triangles make up the large triangle?

Ⓐ 2

Ⓑ 3

Ⓒ 4

Ⓓ 5

28 Which card has 4 fish on it?

    A   B   C   D

Ⓐ Card A

Ⓑ Card B

Ⓒ Card C

Ⓓ Card D

29 What is being found below?

Ⓐ height

Ⓑ length

Ⓒ volume

Ⓓ weight

30 Which glass is empty?

Ⓐ Glass A

Ⓑ Glass B

Ⓒ Glass C

Ⓓ Glass D

31 What shape is shown below?

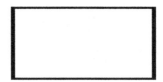

   Ⓐ circle

   Ⓑ rectangle

   Ⓒ square

   Ⓓ triangle

32 What is 6 − 2?

   Ⓐ 2

   Ⓑ 3

   Ⓒ 4

   Ⓓ 5

33 What do all cones have?

Ⓐ no round faces

Ⓑ 1 round face

Ⓒ 2 round faces

Ⓓ 3 round faces

34 What number do the blocks show?

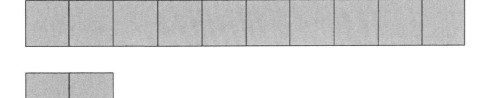

Ⓐ 12

Ⓑ 18

Ⓒ 20

Ⓓ 22

35 How many strawberries are there?

Ⓐ 7

Ⓑ 8

Ⓒ 9

Ⓓ 10

36 Which is equal to 8?

Ⓐ 6 + 1

Ⓑ 6 + 2

Ⓒ 6 + 3

Ⓓ 6 + 4

Practice Test 3

Session 1

Instructions

Read each question carefully.

Each question has four answer choices.

Fill in the circle for the correct answer.

1 How many flowers are there?

(A) 3

(B) 4

(C) 5

(D) 6

2 How long is the saw?

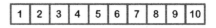

(A) 7 units

(B) 8 units

(C) 9 units

(D) 10 units

3   Where is the tent?

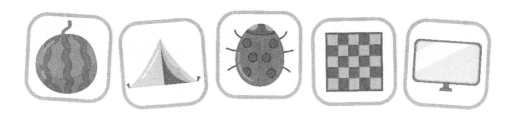

Ⓐ   first

Ⓑ   second

Ⓒ   third

Ⓓ   fourth

4   Which number is 1 less than 87?

Ⓐ   83

Ⓑ   86

Ⓒ   88

Ⓓ   89

5 Sam has 6 shells.

He throws 3 shells away. How many are left?

Ⓐ 2 shells

Ⓑ 3 shells

Ⓒ 4 shells

Ⓓ 5 shells

6 Which item is the shortest?

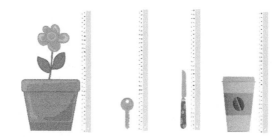

Ⓐ pot

Ⓑ key

Ⓒ knife

Ⓓ cup

7   Which shape is a cone?

Ⓐ

Ⓑ

Ⓒ

Ⓓ

8   Which number has 1 ten and 8 ones?

Ⓐ   9

Ⓑ   10

Ⓒ   18

Ⓓ   19

9   How many of the animals below are monkeys?

Ⓐ 2

Ⓑ 3

Ⓒ 4

Ⓓ 5

10   What does the picture show?

Ⓐ 2 + 2 = 4

Ⓑ 3 + 2 = 5

Ⓒ 3 + 3 = 6

Ⓓ 2 + 5 = 7

11 What are all the items shaped like?

Ⓐ circles

Ⓑ rectangles

Ⓒ squares

Ⓓ triangles

12 What is 3 + 5?

Ⓐ 6

Ⓑ 7

Ⓒ 8

Ⓓ 9

Practice Test 3

Session 2

Instructions

Read each question carefully.

Each question has four answer choices.

Fill in the circle for the correct answer.

13 What number is added to 2 to make 10?

Ⓐ 6

Ⓑ 7

Ⓒ 8

Ⓓ 9

14 A school has 5 buses.

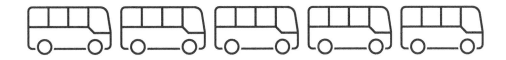

The school buys 2 more. How many buses are there?

Ⓐ 7

Ⓑ 8

Ⓒ 9

Ⓓ 10

15 What number is missing?

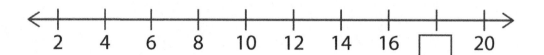

(A) 15

(B) 17

(C) 18

(D) 19

16 Which set has 6 ducks?

17 How many fish and shells are there?

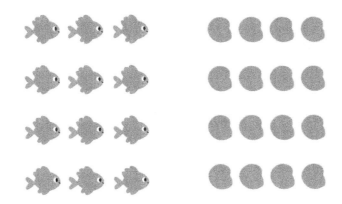

(A) no shells or fish

(B) more shells than fish

(C) less shells than fish

(D) equal shells and fish

18 What number comes right after 39?

(A) 30

(B) 40

(C) 50

(D) 60

19 What is this showing about the flower?

Ⓐ age

Ⓑ color

Ⓒ height

Ⓓ weight

20 How is a triangle different from a square?

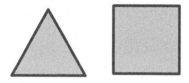

Ⓐ It has less sides.

Ⓑ It has more sides.

Ⓒ It has longer sides.

Ⓓ It has shorter sides.

21 Which item is first in the line below?

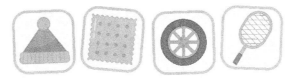

Ⓐ hat

Ⓑ pillow

Ⓒ wheel

Ⓓ bat

22 Which of these shows 7 drums?

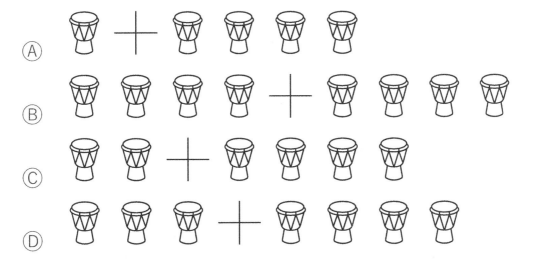

23 What shape is the tennis ball?

Ⓐ cone

Ⓑ cylinder

Ⓒ cube

Ⓓ sphere

24 Which two numbers make 9?

Ⓐ 1 and 7

Ⓑ 2 and 5

Ⓒ 3 and 4

Ⓓ 4 and 5

Practice Test 3

Session 3

Instructions

Read each question carefully.

Each question has four answer choices.

Fill in the circle for the correct answer.

25 There are 5 fish in a bowl. Joe takes 3 away.

How many fish are left?

(A) 1

(B) 2

(C) 3

(D) 4

26 How many of the fruits below are bananas?

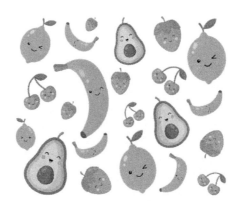

(A) 2

(B) 3

(C) 4

(D) 5

27 What do the three squares combine to make?

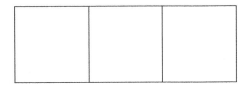

Ⓐ square

Ⓑ rectangle

Ⓒ triangle

Ⓓ circle

28 Which card has 3 turtles on it?

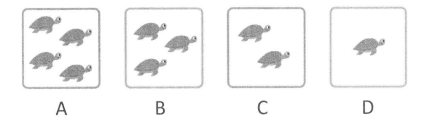

A   B   C   D

Ⓐ Card A

Ⓑ Card B

Ⓒ Card C

Ⓓ Card D

29 What is being found about the jelly?

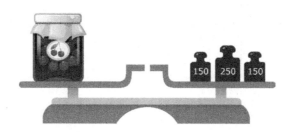

Ⓐ how long it is

Ⓑ how tall it is

Ⓒ how heavy it is

Ⓓ how full it is

30 What does this show about the apple?

Ⓐ It is heavier.

Ⓑ It is lighter.

Ⓒ It is larger.

Ⓓ It is longer.

31   Which shape is a triangle?

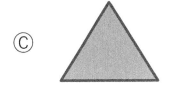

32   What is 6 + 2?

Ⓐ 7

Ⓑ 8

Ⓒ 9

Ⓓ 10

33 How many round faces does a cylinder have?

(A)   0

(B)   1

(C)   2

(D)   3

34 What do the blocks show?

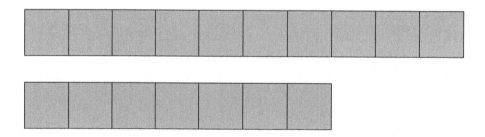

(A)   1 ten + 7 ones

(B)   1 ten + 17 ones

(C)   10 tens + 7 ones

(D)   10 tens + 17 ones

35 How many candles are there?

(A) 10

(B) 12

(C) 15

(D) 18

36 Which is equal to 5?

(A) 2 + 2

(B) 2 + 3

(C) 4 + 2

(D) 4 + 3

Practice Test 4

Session 1

Instructions

Read each question carefully.

Each question has four answer choices.

Fill in the circle for the correct answer.

1   How many cakes are there?

(A)   6

(B)   8

(C)   10

(D)   12

2   How tall is the bear?

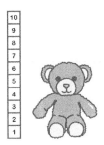

(A)   5 units

(B)   6 units

(C)   7 units

(D)   8 units

3 Where is the clock?

Ⓐ first

Ⓑ second

Ⓒ fourth

Ⓓ fifth

4 Which number is 1 more than 79?

Ⓐ 60

Ⓑ 70

Ⓒ 80

Ⓓ 90

5 Tina has 6 toy trains.

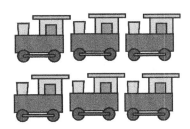

She gives 1 train to a friend. How many are left?

Ⓐ   2 trains

Ⓑ   3 trains

Ⓒ   4 trains

Ⓓ   5 trains

6 Which item is the tallest?

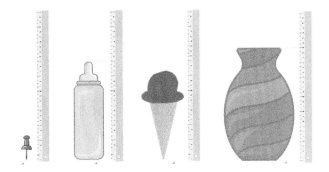

Ⓐ   pin

Ⓑ   bottle

Ⓒ   ice cream

Ⓓ   vase

7   Which shape is a cylinder?

Ⓐ

Ⓑ

Ⓒ

Ⓓ

8   Which number is shown?

1 ten + 3 ones

Ⓐ   4

Ⓑ   13

Ⓒ   14

Ⓓ   30

9 How many of the animals below are frogs?

Ⓐ 3

Ⓑ 4

Ⓒ 5

Ⓓ 6

10 What does the picture show?

Ⓐ $3 - 2 = 1$

Ⓑ $5 - 2 = 3$

Ⓒ $6 - 2 = 4$

Ⓓ $7 - 2 = 5$

11 What are the items shaped like?

Ⓐ circles

Ⓑ rectangles

Ⓒ squares

Ⓓ triangles

12 What is 3 + 3?

Ⓐ 4

Ⓑ 5

Ⓒ 6

Ⓓ 7

Practice Test 4

Session 2

Instructions

Read each question carefully.

Each question has four answer choices.

Fill in the circle for the correct answer.

13 What number is added to 4 to make 10?

Ⓐ 2

Ⓑ 4

Ⓒ 6

Ⓓ 8

14 There are 5 pots on a shelf.

Kim added 3 more pots. How many pots are there?

Ⓐ 7

Ⓑ 8

Ⓒ 9

Ⓓ 10

15 What numbers are missing?

Ⓐ 2 and 5

Ⓑ 2 and 6

Ⓒ 4 and 5

Ⓓ 4 and 6

16 Which set has 10 bells?

Ⓐ

Ⓑ

Ⓒ

Ⓓ

17 In which set are there less suns than clouds?

18 What number comes next?

$$42, 43, 44, \_\_\_\_\_$$

Ⓐ 45

Ⓑ 46

Ⓒ 47

Ⓓ 48

19 What is this showing about the crayon?

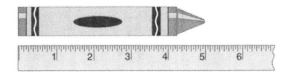

Ⓐ age

Ⓑ color

Ⓒ length

Ⓓ weight

20 What do all triangles have?

Ⓐ no sides

Ⓑ 3 sides

Ⓒ 4 sides

Ⓓ 6 sides

21 Which item is fifth in the line below?

(A) table

(B) book

(C) wool

(D) leaf

22 What is equal to 8?

(A) 5 + 1

(B) 5 + 2

(C) 5 + 3

(D) 5 + 4

23 What shape is the candle?

(A) cone

(B) cylinder

(C) cube

(D) sphere

24 Which number is 2 less than 7?

(A) 3

(B) 4

(C) 5

(D) 6

Practice Test 4

Session 3

Instructions

Read each question carefully.

Each question has four answer choices.

Fill in the circle for the correct answer.

25 There are 5 lemons. Lola uses 3.

How many lemons are left?

(A) 2

(B) 4

(C) 6

(D) 8

26 How many of the shapes below are triangles?

(A) 2

(B) 3

(C) 4

(D) 5

27 What do the two triangles combine to make?

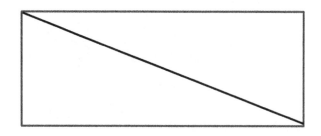

(A) square

(B) rectangle

(C) triangle

(D) circle

28 Which row has 7 hats in it?

(A) Row A

(B) Row B

(C) Row C

(D) Row D

29 Which of these tells how much the bucket holds?

Ⓐ cost

Ⓑ height

Ⓒ length

Ⓓ volume

30 What does this show about the rock?

Ⓐ It is heavier.

Ⓑ It is lighter.

Ⓒ It is smaller.

Ⓓ It is shorter.

31 Which shape is a circle?

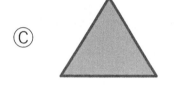

32 What is 5 + 4?

Ⓐ 7

Ⓑ 8

Ⓒ 9

Ⓓ 10

33 Which shape has square faces?

Ⓐ

Ⓑ

Ⓒ

Ⓓ

34 What number do the blocks show?

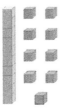

Ⓐ 19

Ⓑ 29

Ⓒ 90

Ⓓ 99

35 Some trucks are shown below.

How many trucks are there?

(A) 7

(B) 8

(C) 9

(D) 10

36 Which is equal to 6?

(A) 2 + 2

(B) 3 + 3

(C) 4 + 4

(D) 5 + 5

ANSWER KEY

Introducing the B.E.S.T. Standards for Mathematics

In 2020, the state of Florida introduced the B.E.S.T. standards. The standards describe the skills and knowledge that students are expected to have. The new standards will be fully introduced by 2022-2023 and the state tests will assess these new standards beginning with the 2022-2023 school year.

About the B.E.S.T. Standards for Mathematics

The B.E.S.T. Standards for Kindergarten are divided into five strands, or topics. These are listed below.

- Number Sense and Operations
- Algebraic Reasoning
- Measurement
- Geometric Reasoning
- Data Analysis and Probability

Within each strand, there is a specific benchmark that each question is testing. The answer key that follows lists the benchmark for each question. Use the skills listed to identify skills that the student is lacking. Then target revision and instruction accordingly.

Practice Test 1, Session 1

Question	Answer	Benchmark
1	C	MA.K.NSO.1.1 Given a group of up to 20 objects, count the number of objects in that group and represent the number of objects with a written numeral. State the number of objects in a rearrangement of that group without recounting.
2	C	MA.K.M.1.3 Express the length of an object, up to 20 units long, as a whole number of lengths by laying non-standard objects end to end with no gaps or overlaps.
3	C	MA.K.NSO.1.3 Identify positions of objects within a sequence using the words "first," "second," "third," "fourth" or "fifth."
4	B	MA.K.NSO.2.1 Recite the number names to 100 by ones and by tens. Starting at a given number, count forward within 100 and backward within 20.
5	B	MA.K.AR.1.3 Solve addition and subtraction real-world problems using objects, drawings or equations to represent the problem.
6	A	MA.K.M.1.2 Directly compare two objects that have an attribute which can be measured in common. Express the comparison using language to describe the difference.
7	D	MA.K.GR.1.1 Identify two- and three-dimensional figures regardless of their size or orientation. Figures are limited to circles, triangles, rectangles, squares, spheres, cubes, cones and cylinders.
8	C	MA.K.NSO.2.2 Represent whole numbers from 10 to 20, using a unit of ten and a group of ones, with objects, drawings and expressions or equations.
9	B	MA.K.DP.1.1 Collect and sort objects into categories and compare the categories by counting the objects in each category. Report the results verbally, with a written numeral or with drawings.
10	B	MA.K.AR.2.1 Explain why addition or subtraction equations are true using objects or drawings.
11	B	MA.K.GR.1.4 Find real-world objects that can be modeled by a given two- or three-dimensional figure. Figures are limited to circles, triangles, rectangles, squares, spheres, cubes, cones and cylinders.
12	B	MA.K.NSO.3.1 Explore addition of two whole numbers from 0 to 10, and related subtraction facts.

Practice Test 1, Session 2

Question	Answer	Benchmark
13	B	MA.K.AR.1.1 For any number from 1 to 9, find the number that makes 10 when added to the given number.
14	B	MA.K.AR.1.3 Solve addition and subtraction real-world problems using objects, drawings or equations to represent the problem.
15	C	MA.K.NSO.2.3 Locate, order and compare numbers from 0 to 20 using the number line and terms less than, equal to or greater than.
16	C	MA.K.NSO.1.2 Given a number from 0 to 20, count out that many objects.
17	D	MA.K.NSO.1.4 Compare the number of objects from 0 to 20 in two groups using the terms less than, equal to or greater than.
18	C	MA.K.NSO.2.1 Recite the number names to 100 by ones and by tens. Starting at a given number, count forward within 100 and backward within 20.
19	B	MA.K.M.1.1 Identify the attributes of a single object that can be measured such as length, volume or weight.
20	A	MA.K.GR.1.2 Compare two-dimensional figures based on their similarities, differences and positions. Sort two-dimensional figures based on their similarities and differences.
21	A	MA.K.NSO.1.3 Identify positions of objects within a sequence using the words "first," "second," "third," "fourth" or "fifth."
22	C	MA.K.AR.1.2 Given a number from 0 to 10, find the different ways it can be represented as the sum of two numbers.
23	B	MA.K.GR.1.4 Find real-world objects that can be modeled by a given two- or three-dimensional figure. Figures are limited to circles, triangles, rectangles, squares, spheres, cubes, cones and cylinders.
24	B	MA.K.NSO.3.2 Add two one-digit whole numbers with sums from 0 to 10 and subtract using related facts with procedural reliability.

Practice Test 1, Session 3

Question	Answer	Benchmark
25	B	MA.K.NSO.3.1 Explore addition of two whole numbers from 0 to 10, and related subtraction facts.
26	B	MA.K.DP.1.1 Collect and sort objects into categories and compare the categories by counting the objects in each category. Report the results verbally, with a written numeral or with drawings.
27	A	MA.K.GR.1.5 Combine two-dimensional figures to form a given composite figure. Figures used to form a composite shape are limited to triangles, rectangles and squares.
28	C	MA.K.NSO.1.2 Given a number from 0 to 20, count out that many objects.
29	C	MA.K.M.1.1 Identify the attributes of a single object that can be measured such as length, volume or weight.
30	C	MA.K.M.1.2 Directly compare two objects that have an attribute which can be measured in common. Express the comparison using language to describe the difference.
31	C	MA.K.GR.1.1 Identify two- and three-dimensional figures regardless of their size or orientation. Figures are limited to circles, triangles, rectangles, squares, spheres, cubes, cones and cylinders.
32	B	MA.K.NSO.3.2 Add two one-digit whole numbers with sums from 0 to 10 and subtract using related facts with procedural reliability.
33	D	MA.K.GR.1.3 Compare three-dimensional figures based on their similarities, differences and positions. Sort three-dimensional figures based on their similarities and differences.
34	B	MA.K.NSO.2.2 Represent whole numbers from 10 to 20, using a unit of ten and a group of ones, with objects, drawings and expressions or equations.
35	C	MA.K.NSO.1.1 Given a group of up to 20 objects, count the number of objects in that group and represent the number of objects with a written numeral. State the number of objects in a rearrangement of that group without recounting.
36	D	MA.K.AR.1.2 Given a number from 0 to 10, find the different ways it can be represented as the sum of two numbers.

Practice Test 2, Session 1

Question	Answer	Benchmark
1	C	MA.K.NSO.1.1 Given a group of up to 20 objects, count the number of objects in that group and represent the number of objects with a written numeral. State the number of objects in a rearrangement of that group without recounting.
2	B	MA.K.M.1.3 Express the length of an object, up to 20 units long, as a whole number of lengths by laying non-standard objects end to end with no gaps or overlaps.
3	D	MA.K.NSO.1.3 Identify positions of objects within a sequence using the words "first," "second," "third," "fourth" or "fifth."
4	B	MA.K.NSO.2.1 Recite the number names to 100 by ones and by tens. Starting at a given number, count forward within 100 and backward within 20.
5	C	MA.K.AR.1.3 Solve addition and subtraction real-world problems using objects, drawings or equations to represent the problem.
6	B	MA.K.M.1.2 Directly compare two objects that have an attribute which can be measured in common. Express the comparison using language to describe the difference.
7	C	MA.K.GR.1.1 Identify two- and three-dimensional figures regardless of their size or orientation. Figures are limited to circles, triangles, rectangles, squares, spheres, cubes, cones and cylinders.
8	B	MA.K.NSO.2.2 Represent whole numbers from 10 to 20, using a unit of ten and a group of ones, with objects, drawings and expressions or equations.
9	C	MA.K.DP.1.1 Collect and sort objects into categories and compare the categories by counting the objects in each category. Report the results verbally, with a written numeral or with drawings.
10	C	MA.K.AR.2.1 Explain why addition or subtraction equations are true using objects or drawings.
11	A	MA.K.GR.1.4 Find real-world objects that can be modeled by a given two- or three-dimensional figure. Figures are limited to circles, triangles, rectangles, squares, spheres, cubes, cones and cylinders.
12	C	MA.K.NSO.3.1 Explore addition of two whole numbers from 0 to 10, and related subtraction facts.

Practice Test 2, Session 2

Question	Answer	Benchmark
13	C	MA.K.AR.1.1 For any number from 1 to 9, find the number that makes 10 when added to the given number.
14	A	MA.K.AR.1.3 Solve addition and subtraction real-world problems using objects, drawings or equations to represent the problem.
15	B	MA.K.NSO.2.3 Locate, order and compare numbers from 0 to 20 using the number line and terms less than, equal to or greater than.
16	D	MA.K.NSO.1.2 Given a number from 0 to 20, count out that many objects.
17	C	MA.K.NSO.1.4 Compare the number of objects from 0 to 20 in two groups using the terms less than, equal to or greater than.
18	B	MA.K.NSO.2.1 Recite the number names to 100 by ones and by tens. Starting at a given number, count forward within 100 and backward within 20.
19	B	MA.K.M.1.1 Identify the attributes of a single object that can be measured such as length, volume or weight.
20	A	MA.K.GR.1.2 Compare two-dimensional figures based on their similarities, differences and positions. Sort two-dimensional figures based on their similarities and differences.
21	C	MA.K.NSO.1.3 Identify positions of objects within a sequence using the words "first," "second," "third," "fourth" or "fifth."
22	C	MA.K.AR.1.2 Given a number from 0 to 10, find the different ways it can be represented as the sum of two numbers.
23	B	MA.K.GR.1.4 Find real-world objects that can be modeled by a given two- or three-dimensional figure. Figures are limited to circles, triangles, rectangles, squares, spheres, cubes, cones and cylinders.
24	C	MA.K.NSO.3.2 Add two one-digit whole numbers with sums from 0 to 10 and subtract using related facts with procedural reliability.

Practice Test 2, Session 3

Question	Answer	Benchmark
25	C	MA.K.NSO.3.1 Explore addition of two whole numbers from 0 to 10, and related subtraction facts.
26	A	MA.K.DP.1.1 Collect and sort objects into categories and compare the categories by counting the objects in each category. Report the results verbally, with a written numeral or with drawings.
27	C	MA.K.GR.1.5 Combine two-dimensional figures to form a given composite figure. Figures used to form a composite shape are limited to triangles, rectangles and squares.
28	B	MA.K.NSO.1.2 Given a number from 0 to 20, count out that many objects.
29	C	MA.K.M.1.1 Identify the attributes of a single object that can be measured such as length, volume or weight.
30	D	MA.K.M.1.2 Directly compare two objects that have an attribute which can be measured in common. Express the comparison using language to describe the difference.
31	B	MA.K.GR.1.1 Identify two- and three-dimensional figures regardless of their size or orientation. Figures are limited to circles, triangles, rectangles, squares, spheres, cubes, cones and cylinders.
32	C	MA.K.NSO.3.2 Add two one-digit whole numbers with sums from 0 to 10 and subtract using related facts with procedural reliability.
33	B	MA.K.GR.1.3 Compare three-dimensional figures based on their similarities, differences and positions. Sort three-dimensional figures based on their similarities and differences.
34	A	MA.K.NSO.2.2 Represent whole numbers from 10 to 20, using a unit of ten and a group of ones, with objects, drawings and expressions or equations.
35	B	MA.K.NSO.1.1 Given a group of up to 20 objects, count the number of objects in that group and represent the number of objects with a written numeral. State the number of objects in a rearrangement of that group without recounting.
36	B	MA.K.AR.1.2 Given a number from 0 to 10, find the different ways it can be represented as the sum of two numbers.

Practice Test 3, Session 1

Question	Answer	Benchmark
1	C	MA.K.NSO.1.1 Given a group of up to 20 objects, count the number of objects in that group and represent the number of objects with a written numeral. State the number of objects in a rearrangement of that group without recounting.
2	A	MA.K.M.1.3 Express the length of an object, up to 20 units long, as a whole number of lengths by laying non-standard objects end to end with no gaps or overlaps.
3	B	MA.K.NSO.1.3 Identify positions of objects within a sequence using the words "first," "second," "third," "fourth" or "fifth."
4	B	MA.K.NSO.2.1 Recite the number names to 100 by ones and by tens. Starting at a given number, count forward within 100 and backward within 20.
5	B	MA.K.AR.1.3 Solve addition and subtraction real-world problems using objects, drawings or equations to represent the problem.
6	B	MA.K.M.1.2 Directly compare two objects that have an attribute which can be measured in common. Express the comparison using language to describe the difference.
7	D	MA.K.GR.1.1 Identify two- and three-dimensional figures regardless of their size or orientation. Figures are limited to circles, triangles, rectangles, squares, spheres, cubes, cones and cylinders.
8	C	MA.K.NSO.2.2 Represent whole numbers from 10 to 20, using a unit of ten and a group of ones, with objects, drawings and expressions or equations.
9	A	MA.K.DP.1.1 Collect and sort objects into categories and compare the categories by counting the objects in each category. Report the results verbally, with a written numeral or with drawings.
10	B	MA.K.AR.2.1 Explain why addition or subtraction equations are true using objects or drawings.
11	D	MA.K.GR.1.4 Find real-world objects that can be modeled by a given two- or three-dimensional figure. Figures are limited to circles, triangles, rectangles, squares, spheres, cubes, cones and cylinders.
12	C	MA.K.NSO.3.1 Explore addition of two whole numbers from 0 to 10, and related subtraction facts.

Practice Test 3, Session 2

Question	Answer	Benchmark
13	C	MA.K.AR.1.1 For any number from 1 to 9, find the number that makes 10 when added to the given number.
14	A	MA.K.AR.1.3 Solve addition and subtraction real-world problems using objects, drawings or equations to represent the problem.
15	C	MA.K.NSO.2.3 Locate, order and compare numbers from 0 to 20 using the number line and terms less than, equal to or greater than.
16	C	MA.K.NSO.1.2 Given a number from 0 to 20, count out that many objects.
17	B	MA.K.NSO.1.4 Compare the number of objects from 0 to 20 in two groups using the terms less than, equal to or greater than.
18	B	MA.K.NSO.2.1 Recite the number names to 100 by ones and by tens. Starting at a given number, count forward within 100 and backward within 20.
19	C	MA.K.M.1.1 Identify the attributes of a single object that can be measured such as length, volume or weight.
20	A	MA.K.GR.1.2 Compare two-dimensional figures based on their similarities, differences and positions. Sort two-dimensional figures based on their similarities and differences.
21	A	MA.K.NSO.1.3 Identify positions of objects within a sequence using the words "first," "second," "third," "fourth" or "fifth."
22	D	MA.K.AR.1.2 Given a number from 0 to 10, find the different ways it can be represented as the sum of two numbers.
23	D	MA.K.GR.1.4 Find real-world objects that can be modeled by a given two- or three-dimensional figure. Figures are limited to circles, triangles, rectangles, squares, spheres, cubes, cones and cylinders.
24	D	MA.K.NSO.3.2 Add two one-digit whole numbers with sums from 0 to 10 and subtract using related facts with procedural reliability.

Practice Test 3, Session 3

Question	Answer	Benchmark
25	B	MA.K.NSO.3.1 Explore addition of two whole numbers from 0 to 10, and related subtraction facts.
26	D	MA.K.DP.1.1 Collect and sort objects into categories and compare the categories by counting the objects in each category. Report the results verbally, with a written numeral or with drawings.
27	B	MA.K.GR.1.5 Combine two-dimensional figures to form a given composite figure. Figures used to form a composite shape are limited to triangles, rectangles and squares.
28	B	MA.K.NSO.1.2 Given a number from 0 to 20, count out that many objects.
29	C	MA.K.M.1.1 Identify the attributes of a single object that can be measured such as length, volume or weight.
30	B	MA.K.M.1.2 Directly compare two objects that have an attribute which can be measured in common. Express the comparison using language to describe the difference.
31	C	MA.K.GR.1.1 Identify two- and three-dimensional figures regardless of their size or orientation. Figures are limited to circles, triangles, rectangles, squares, spheres, cubes, cones and cylinders.
32	B	MA.K.NSO.3.2 Add two one-digit whole numbers with sums from 0 to 10 and subtract using related facts with procedural reliability.
33	C	MA.K.GR.1.3 Compare three-dimensional figures based on their similarities, differences and positions. Sort three-dimensional figures based on their similarities and differences.
34	A	MA.K.NSO.2.2 Represent whole numbers from 10 to 20, using a unit of ten and a group of ones, with objects, drawings and expressions or equations.
35	C	MA.K.NSO.1.1 Given a group of up to 20 objects, count the number of objects in that group and represent the number of objects with a written numeral. State the number of objects in a rearrangement of that group without recounting.
36	B	MA.K.AR.1.2 Given a number from 0 to 10, find the different ways it can be represented as the sum of two numbers.

Practice Test 4, Session 1

Question	Answer	Benchmark
1	C	MA.K.NSO.1.1 Given a group of up to 20 objects, count the number of objects in that group and represent the number of objects with a written numeral. State the number of objects in a rearrangement of that group without recounting.
2	B	MA.K.M.1.3 Express the length of an object, up to 20 units long, as a whole number of lengths by laying non-standard objects end to end with no gaps or overlaps.
3	D	MA.K.NSO.1.3 Identify positions of objects within a sequence using the words "first," "second," "third," "fourth" or "fifth."
4	C	MA.K.NSO.2.1 Recite the number names to 100 by ones and by tens. Starting at a given number, count forward within 100 and backward within 20.
5	D	MA.K.AR.1.3 Solve addition and subtraction real-world problems using objects, drawings or equations to represent the problem.
6	D	MA.K.M.1.2 Directly compare two objects that have an attribute which can be measured in common. Express the comparison using language to describe the difference.
7	A	MA.K.GR.1.1 Identify two- and three-dimensional figures regardless of their size or orientation. Figures are limited to circles, triangles, rectangles, squares, spheres, cubes, cones and cylinders.
8	B	MA.K.NSO.2.2 Represent whole numbers from 10 to 20, using a unit of ten and a group of ones, with objects, drawings and expressions or equations.
9	B	MA.K.DP.1.1 Collect and sort objects into categories and compare the categories by counting the objects in each category. Report the results verbally, with a written numeral or with drawings.
10	B	MA.K.AR.2.1 Explain why addition or subtraction equations are true using objects or drawings.
11	B	MA.K.GR.1.4 Find real-world objects that can be modeled by a given two- or three-dimensional figure. Figures are limited to circles, triangles, rectangles, squares, spheres, cubes, cones and cylinders.
12	C	MA.K.NSO.3.1 Explore addition of two whole numbers from 0 to 10, and related subtraction facts.

Practice Test 4, Session 2

Question	Answer	Benchmark
13	C	MA.K.AR.1.1 For any number from 1 to 9, find the number that makes 10 when added to the given number.
14	B	MA.K.AR.1.3 Solve addition and subtraction real-world problems using objects, drawings or equations to represent the problem.
15	B	MA.K.NSO.2.3 Locate, order and compare numbers from 0 to 20 using the number line and terms less than, equal to or greater than.
16	C	MA.K.NSO.1.2 Given a number from 0 to 20, count out that many objects.
17	B	MA.K.NSO.1.4 Compare the number of objects from 0 to 20 in two groups using the terms less than, equal to or greater than.
18	A	MA.K.NSO.2.1 Recite the number names to 100 by ones and by tens. Starting at a given number, count forward within 100 and backward within 20.
19	C	MA.K.M.1.1 Identify the attributes of a single object that can be measured such as length, volume or weight.
20	B	MA.K.GR.1.2 Compare two-dimensional figures based on their similarities, differences and positions. Sort two-dimensional figures based on their similarities and differences.
21	D	MA.K.NSO.1.3 Identify positions of objects within a sequence using the words "first," "second," "third," "fourth" or "fifth."
22	C	MA.K.AR.1.2 Given a number from 0 to 10, find the different ways it can be represented as the sum of two numbers.
23	B	MA.K.GR.1.4 Find real-world objects that can be modeled by a given two- or three-dimensional figure. Figures are limited to circles, triangles, rectangles, squares, spheres, cubes, cones and cylinders.
24	C	MA.K.NSO.3.2 Add two one-digit whole numbers with sums from 0 to 10 and subtract using related facts with procedural reliability.

Practice Test 4, Session 3

Question	Answer	Benchmark
25	A	MA.K.NSO.3.1 Explore addition of two whole numbers from 0 to 10, and related subtraction facts.
26	C	MA.K.DP.1.1 Collect and sort objects into categories and compare the categories by counting the objects in each category. Report the results verbally, with a written numeral or with drawings.
27	B	MA.K.GR.1.5 Combine two-dimensional figures to form a given composite figure. Figures used to form a composite shape are limited to triangles, rectangles and squares.
28	C	MA.K.NSO.1.2 Given a number from 0 to 20, count out that many objects.
29	D	MA.K.M.1.1 Identify the attributes of a single object that can be measured such as length, volume or weight.
30	A	MA.K.M.1.2 Directly compare two objects that have an attribute which can be measured in common. Express the comparison using language to describe the difference.
31	A	MA.K.GR.1.1 Identify two- and three-dimensional figures regardless of their size or orientation. Figures are limited to circles, triangles, rectangles, squares, spheres, cubes, cones and cylinders.
32	C	MA.K.NSO.3.2 Add two one-digit whole numbers with sums from 0 to 10 and subtract using related facts with procedural reliability.
33	B	MA.K.GR.1.3 Compare three-dimensional figures based on their similarities, differences and positions. Sort three-dimensional figures based on their similarities and differences.
34	A	MA.K.NSO.2.2 Represent whole numbers from 10 to 20, using a unit of ten and a group of ones, with objects, drawings and expressions or equations.
35	C	MA.K.NSO.1.1 Given a group of up to 20 objects, count the number of objects in that group and represent the number of objects with a written numeral. State the number of objects in a rearrangement of that group without recounting.
36	B	MA.K.AR.1.2 Given a number from 0 to 10, find the different ways it can be represented as the sum of two numbers.

Made in United States
Orlando, FL
09 May 2025

61170291R00057